YOUR KNOWLEDGE HAS VALUE

Agnetha Hinz

The Concept of Music in Robert Henryson's "Orpheus and Eurydice"

GRIN Publishing

Bibliographic information published by the German National Library:

The German National Library lists this publication in the National Bibliography; detailed bibliographic data are available on the Internet at http://dnb.dnb.de .

Imprint:

Copyright © 2012 GRIN Verlag, Open Publishing GmbH
Print and binding: Books on Demand GmbH, Norderstedt Germany
ISBN: 978-3-668-01242-4

This book at GRIN:

http://www.grin.com/en/e-book/302899/the-concept-of-music-in-robert-henryson-s-orpheus-and-eurydice

Freie Universität Berlin

English Philology

- Medieval English Literatures II -

Research paper

"The concept of music in Robert Henryson's Orpheus and Eurydice"

SoSe 2012

Agnetha Hinz

2. Fachsemester

Table of Content

1. Introduction 2

2. The concept of music 3

    2.1. Music in the Middle Ages 3

    2.2. Music in Orpheus and Eurydice 4

3. Conclusion 7

Works cited 8

1. Introduction

"Music, through the sweetness of its melody, brings pleasure and comfort to the soul."

This citation by Nigel Wilkin in "Music in the Age of Chaucer" (XIV) ascribes a special own form of power to music; the power to affect someone's soul. Also in the poem of *Orpheus and Eurydice* by the Scottish poet Robert Henryson (c. 1425 – c. 1506), music plays a decisive role and implies a special power to the protagonist. The poem, which approximately was written in the late fifteenth century, leans on the Greek myth of Orpheus.

King Orpheus, who is introduced as the grandson of Memoria and Jupiter, the son of the "michty god Phebuss" (Henryson line 62) and the muse Caliope, "that madin mervalouss,/ The ferd sistir, of all musik maistress" (Henryson lines 43-44), gains his bond to music through his mother's milk, quod vide "gart him souk of hir twa paupis quhyte/ The sueit lecour of all musik perfyte" (Henryson lines 69-70).

Henryson describes Orpheus as "fair and wyse,/ Gentill and gud, full of liberalitie" (Henryson lines 64-65). His "noble fame" (Henryson line 73) was extensive, so that the queen of "Trace", called Eurydice, heard about him, too. They get married and live their life full of happiness, pleasure and enjoyment.

One morning in May, the queen takes a walk and is ambushed by a herdsman. She flees and steps on a poisonous snake. When Orpheus heard that his wife is taken with "the phary" (Henryson line 119), he "inflammit all in yre" (Henryson line 120) and goes off into the wilderness.

Orpheus starts to travel the planets to find Eurydice. After his unsuccessful journey, he tries to find her in Heaven. He fails again and decides to look for her in hell. He passes various denizens of the underworld and finally he finds Eurydice, plays his harp in front of Pluto and Proserpene, who build the hellish court and was given permission to leave hell with his wife on condition not to turn around while leaving, otherwise Eurydice has to stay in Hell forever. Although this condition is hard, Orpheus is willing to risk it. When "thay almost come to the outwart port" (Henryson line 386), Orpheus forgets about the condition, turns around and loses all.

2. The concept of music

2.1. Music in the Middle Ages

One definition for the term 'music' in the Middle Ages was given by Augustine of Hippo, a Latin philosopher and theologian:

"Musica est scientia bene modulandi."

This can be translated as "Music is the science to keep the metre", which perfectly describes the medieval meaning of music in these times, because "music was primarily the science of numbers, the proportions that regulate sounds among themselves." ("Encyclopedia of the Middle Ages 994")

At universities music was taught next to arithmetic, geometry and astronomy, which altogether formed "the quadrivium" ("Encyclopedia of the Middle Ages" 994) and was transmitted in different types; the monophonic and orally during the early Middle Ages and the polyphonic, which is the addition of "one or more extra voices that [form] consonances or dissonances with the main voice" ("Encyclopedia of the Middle Ages" 994), between the 9th and 12th century. Characteristic of the music in the medieval era are the "linear conceptions [which] continued to dominate music until the end of the Middle Ages" (Stevens, "Words and Music" 2), the verse texts and the beginning of musical notation, which is "probably to be imputed to a political rather than a musical reason." ("Encyclopedia of the Middle Ages" 994)

Until the 13th century music in the Middle Ages was a part of the sacred and political life in forms of "different liturgical actions" ("Encyclopedia of the Middle Ages" 994) such as "processions, worship [and] penitence" ("Encyclopedia of the Middle Ages" 994). Due to the Christianity "music was a *speculum*, a mirror of the Universal Order" (Stevens, "Music and Poetry" 59) by what Christ himself was seen as the supreme musician.

Later on music also affects the secular area of the medieval culture by musicians such as minstrels, who sang about foreign places or romantic stories.

Furthermore people in the Middle Ages tend to ascribe a special power to music, like, in the medical section, the abatement of melancholy or the healing of wounds. Also in literature music plays a symbolic role. In 'The Boke of the Governour' by Sir Thomas Elyot, "music [gives] the young prince an insight into the laws which govern the universe and thereby into the method of good government" (Stevens, "Words and Music" 61). Even in religious traditions music incarnates an essential role in defeating evil power. In the Holy Scripture by

Martin Luther it is written, that King David cured Saul's suffering by playing his harp, see '1 Samuel 16:23': "And it came to pass, when the evil spirit from God was upon Saul, that David took a harp, and played with his hand: so Saul was refreshed, and was well, and the evil spirit departed from him".

Finally it can be said that the concept of music in the Middle Ages results out of severely practical usage and "a fundamental belief in the harmony of the universe, a harmony of the spiritual and physical, the celestial and terrestrial, an eternal harmony of mathematical proportions" (Tatarkiewicz 129).

2.2. Music in Orpheus and Eurydice

The poem of *Orpheus and Eurydice*, an adaption of the Greek story of Orpheus was, as mentioned in the introduction, written by Robert Henryson in the late fifteenth century. In his interpretation Henryson divides into two parts. The first one tells the classical story of Orpheus and Eurydice by concentrating on Orpheus's genealogy, his mourning about the loss of his wife Eurydice and his failure to retrieve her from the underworld. The second one is called the *Moralitas*, which attends to the moral aspects of the story.

The poem consists of 633 lines and serves the rhyme royal stanza, a rhyming stanza of seven lines in iambic pentameter with the rhyme scheme a-b-a-b-b-c-c, which reflects the common form of the narrative metre in the Middle Ages. By that Henryson keeps the linear conception of the medieval literature as well as in music. The only change in style in form of ten-line stanzas takes place from "O dulfull herp with mony dully string,/ Turne all thy mirth and musik in murning" (Henryson lines 134-135) to "King Orpheuss thus with his harp alone/ Sore wepit for his wyf Erudices" (Henryson lines 183-184) to intensify Orpheus's mourning about the loss of Eurydice.

To illustrate the concept of music within the story line, it is necessary to go through the poem by focusing on the music-oriented parts.

In the beginning Henryson thoroughly describes the noble lineage of Orpheus. His grandmother is the goddess Memoria, who married Jupiter and gave birth to the nine Muses, the goddesses of the inspiration of arts, science and literature. One of these muses, Caliope, the mistress of all music is also introduced as Orpheus's mother and the wife of the god Phoebus, Orpheus's father.

4

Due to his divine extraction Orpheus is not only a talented harpist, he is also "a musical theorist who understands the ordered harmonies of *musica mundana*, the music of the spheres." (Kastan 32)

After explaining the familiar background, Henryson starts to tell about Eurydice's invitation to Orpheus, their marriage, the death of Eurydice while fleeing the attack of an uncouth herdsman and finally Orpheus's departure into the wilderness.

First in the woods Orpheus shows his skill in playing his harp, mourning the disappearance of his wife while sitting on a stone. The Power, Orpheus owns due to his music becomes apparent in the lines ,, Him to rejoss, yit playit he a spring,/ Quhill that the fowlis of the wid can sing,/ And treis dansit with thair levis grene " (Henryson lines 144-146). And not only that nature seems to come to life, they also try to avail Orpheus: "Him to devod from his greit womenting;/ Bot all in vane, that wailyeit him no thing" (Henryson lines 147-148).

Afterwards, Orpheus ends his mourning and starts to travel the spheres of the planetary gods to search for his wife. While this journey, in which he fails to find Eurydice, he heard a "hevinly melody and sound" (Henryson line 220). This stanza is the beginning of Orpheus's musical education he gains in the spheres by learning "the mathematical proportions of heavenly harmony" (Kastan 33) and making him a complete musician. In the next two stanzas, Henryson describes that "[t]he *music of the spheres* is itself a teacher to Orpheus of the symbolic of song" (Marvin 62):

Thare leirit he tonis proportionat,
As duplare, triplare, and epetritus;
Enolius, and eik the quadruplait;
Epoddeus, rycht hard and curius;
Off all thir sex, sueite and delicius,
Rycht consonant, fyfe hevinly symphonyss
Componyt ar, as clerkis can devyse.

First diatesserone, full sueit I wiss;
And dyapasone, semple and duplate;
And dyapenty, componyt with the dyss;
Thir makis fyve, of thre multiplicat.
This mirry musik and mellefluat,

5

Compleit and full of nummeris od and evin,

Is causit be the moving of the hevin.

(226-239)

The technical terms Henryson uses "import into the poem a sense of constructedness of Orpheus's art" (Marvin 63) and offer valuable clues to the scholarship of music in the Middle Ages, which was based on arithmetical proportions.

Orpheus's journey finally leads him into hell. Here, Henryson accentuates the celestial power of the protagonist's music again. Orpheus encounters the gatekeeper Cerberus, a three-headed hellhound. By playing his harp, the harmony-bringing medium in this poem, the guard-dog falls asleep and Orpheus continues his way into the underworld. In the next stanza Henryson mentions how Orpheus also played in front of the Three Fates "Electo, Mygra, and Thesaphone" (Henryson line 264) and put them to sleep by playing "a joly spring" (Henryson line 268). When Orpheus encounters Tantalus, who was tortured by thirst, he "saw him suffir neid,/ He tuk his harp and fast on it can clink:/ The wattir stud, and Tantalus gat a drink" (Henryson lines 286-288). On his Orpheus also delivers Ticius from a "grisly grip" (Henryson line 296) by taking "his herp and maid sueit melody;/ The grip is fled, and Titius left his cry" (Henryson lines 301-303). Finally, Orpheus finds Eurydice in hell. Again he plays his music to assure the members of the hellish court of revealing his wife. In the following lines, which illustrate the situation of Orpheus playing in front of the court, Henryson returns to the technical terms of music theory he used to describe Orpheus's musical education in the heavenly spheres:

Than Orpheus befoir Pluto sat doun,

And in his handis quhit his herp can ta,

And playit mony sueit proportioun,

With baiss tonys in ypodorica,

With gemilling in yporlerica;

Quhill at the last, for rewth and grit petie,

Thay weipit soir that cowth him heir or se.

(366-372)

Charmed by his music, "Rodomantus and Proserpina" (Henryson line 308) change their mind and grant the permit to take Eurydice out of hell, which shows that music was Orpheus's only

6

possibility to redeem his beloved from the underworld, even if he loses her all over again by turning around on their way back.

3. Conclusion

Summing up it is to say, that both, the structure of the poem and the story line perfectly match the concept of music in the Middle Ages. Like said before, Henryson keeps the linear conception of the literature in the Middle Ages by using the rhyme royal stanza in iambic pentameter. These rhymes comply with Augustine of Hippo's saying "Musica est scientia bene modulandi" and turn the poem into a harmonic and melodic play, which also could be sung.

As well within the poem Henryson draws upon the medieval concept of music. Orpheus, who is not only the son of gods but also the king of "Trace" fulfils the qualifications of the sacred and political aspects, in which music in the Middle Ages dominated. Due to his journey to the spheres, within which he was educated into a complete musician by learning the mathematical proportions of heavenly harmony, Henryson follows the pattern of „music as a speculum, a mirror of the Universal Order", as well. The delineation of Orpheus's learning process in the spheres, the author phrases the on a theoretic level, which also matches the medieval concept of music as a science. The harp, on which Orpheus produces his celestial sound, is an important element of music in the Middle Ages, as well. Besides the trumpet and the flute, the harp was one of the traditional musical instruments.

The last point remarks the main basic message of the poems. The power of music is the only weapon Orpheus needs to pass through hell to play his harp at last in front of the hellish court until he was given permission to leave the underworld with Eurydice.

Henryson does not mention how or why the denizens of hell, like the Three Fates or Rodomantus and Proserpina, are affected by Orpheus's music, but indeed he does not manipulate their emotions but they are charmed by his music. Thereby Henryson forms the spiritual and celestial belief in a special power of music, out of which, like mentioned above, the medieval concept of music results. Thus, concluding it can be said, that Henryson's poem of Orpheus and Eurydice meets all conditions of the concept of music in the Middle Ages, from its structural composition up to its facts in content.

Works cited

Henryson, Robert. "Orpheus and Eurydice". *The Poems of Robert Henryson*. Ed. Robert L. Kindrick. Kalamazoo, Michigan: Medieval Institute Publications. 1997.

Kastan, David Scott. *The Oxford Encyclopedia of British Literature*. Oxford: Oxford University Press. 2006. Print.

Marvin, Corey J. *Word Outward: Medieval Perspectives on the Entry into Language*. New York: Routledge. 2001. Print.

Stevens, John. *Music and Poetry in the Early Tudor Court*. Cambridge: Cambridge University Press. 1979. Print.

---. *Words and Music in the Middle Ages: Song, Narrative, Dance and Drama, 1050-1350*. Cambridge: Cambridge University Press. 1986. Print.

Tatarkiewicz, Wladyslaw. *History of Aesthetics*. Ed. J. Harrell, C. Barrett, D. Petsch. London: Continuum International Publishing Group. 2005. Print.

Wilkins, Nigel. *Music in the Age of Chaucer*. Cambridge: Boydell & Brewer Ltd. 1979. Print.

Encyclopedia of the Middle Ages: K-Z. Ed. Andre Vauchez. Cambridge: James Clarke & Co. 2000. Print.

The Holy Bible. Translated by Martin Luther. gen. ed. Dallas: International Bible Association. Print.